HODDER ENGLISH 4

War Poetry

In this book you will study poetry written about war. The poems cover a range of conflicts up to Bosnia in the 1990s. Even though the processes and weapons have changed over time, the purposes and outcomes of war remain the same. Through the poetry you will explore some of these purposes and outcomes. You will also be developing your skills as:

SPEAKERS AND LISTENERS

by reading and discussing poems together
by working collaboratively on the poems
by forming and voicing your own opinions

READERS

by reading a wide range of poems and finding comparisons and connections
by reading and re-reading closely to develop your understanding
by exploring the different ways writers use language to convey meaning and
    attitude

WRITERS

by keeping a poetry journal to collect your first impressions
by making notes and writing commentaries
by writing imaginatively in response to some of the poems
by comparing different poets and the way they respond to the issues
by writing more formally for a course work assignment

Look carefully at the images on this page. Describe what you can see in each.

- Explain to a partner which image has the greatest impact on you and why. You might, for instance, consider the different ways in which men and women are portrayed.

- What 'image' of war comes across from each photograph? Where might you see each one of these being used? A history book? An advert? A film poster?

- Select one photograph to explain or analyse for a Speaking and Listening assessment.

- Which of these images could be used for a recruiting poster encouraging people to volunteer? Which image would an anti-war organisation producing leaflets choose?

WAR PHOTOGRAPHER

In his darkroom he is finally alone
with spools of suffering set out in ordered rows.
The only light is red and softly glows,
as though this were a church and he
a priest preparing to intone a Mass.
Belfast. Beirut. Phnom Penh. All flesh is grass.

He has a job to do. Solutions slop in trays
beneath his hands which did not tremble then
though seem to now. Rural England. Home again
to ordinary pain which simple weather can dispel,
to fields which don't explode beneath the feet
of running children in a nightmare heat.

Something is happening. A stranger's features
faintly start to twist before his eyes,
a half-formed ghost. He remembers the cries
of this man's wife, how he sought approval
without words to do what someone must
and how the blood stained into foreign dust.

A hundred agonies in black-and-white
from which his editor will pick out five or six
for Sunday's supplement. The reader's eyeballs prick
with tears between the bath and pre-lunch beers.
From the aeroplane he stares impassively at where
he earns his living and they do not care.

Carol Ann Duffy (1955 -)

- Explain what is happening in this poem. Take it stanza by stanza. What do you notice about the punctuation? What effect does it have?

- Take each sentence in the poem and look in detail at the meaning and impressions given. Explain and discuss the words and their possible connections. For example, the first sentence is:

In his darkroom he is finally alone
with spools of suffering set out in ordered rows.

Think about:

- the connection between spools and darkroom

- why the word suffering was used

- what might be the meaning behind the phrase 'finally alone'

Work through each sentence in this way.

- Write a paragraph explaining how the photographer has been affected by what he has seen. How do you feel about him and the job he does?

- Look back at the page of photographs (p.2). Discuss which images link with lines or phrases in the poem 'War Photographer'.

LANGUAGE OF POETRY

Enjambement – lines of poetry where the structure and meaning carry the reader's eye and ear directly over to the next line without a break. For example:

Solutions slop in trays
beneath his hands which did not tremble then
though seem to now.

Read the following extracts written by war photographer, Don McCullin. What do they say about the work of a war photographer? How is this reflected in the poem you have just read?

1. I don't like going out into the light when I'm in the dark room. I like the consistency of the dark. It keeps me safe. The dark room is a very good place to be. It's a womb. I feel I have everything there that I need. My mind, my emotions, my passions, my chemicals, my papers. My negatives. And my direction. In the dark room I am totally together.

2. Cyprus left me with the beginnings of self-knowledge, and the very beginning of what they call empathy. I found I was able to share other people's emotional experiences, live with them silently, transmit them. I felt I had a particular vision that isolated and homed in on the essence of what was happening, and could see in light, in tones, in details...

What I hoped I had captured in my pictures was an enduring image that would imprint itself on the world's memory. I was looking for a symbol – though I could not then have put it that way – that could stand for the whole story and would have the impact of ritual or religious imagery.

Unreasonable Behaviour by Don McCullin

HELP

POETRY JOURNAL

You may find it helpful to have an exercise book to record your thoughts and feelings for this unit of work and to keep the ideas, notes and reactions that you have. This will be useful when you are asked to do some written course work. As you work through this book poetical terms and techniques will be explained – writing these in your poetry journal will enable you to check on meanings and examples of these techniques whenever you are uncertain. Do not wait to be told to make an entry in your poetry journal, but always date each entry. Use your journal to 'think on paper'. You may find it useful to answer the following questions for each of the poems you study:

- What is the poem saying to me?
- Why was it written in this way?
- What is unusual about the poem?
- What is distinctive about the way words are used?
- What impression do I get from the poem as a whole?
- What do I feel about the poem?

PLATFORM ONE

Holiday squeals, as if all were scrambling for their lives,
Panting aboard the 'Cornish Riviera'.
Then overflow of relief and luggage and children,
Then ducking to smile out as the station moves.

Out there on the platform, under the rain,
Under his rain-cape, helmet and full pack,
Somebody, head bowed reading something,
Doesn't know he's missing his train.

He's completely buried in that book.
He's utterly forgotten where he is.
He's forgotten Paddington, forgotten
Timetables, forgotten the long, rocking

Cradle of a journey into the golden West,
The coach's soft wingbeat – as light
And straight as a dove's flight.
Like a graveyard statue sentry cast

In blackened old bronze. Is he reading poems?
A letter? The burial service? The raindrops
Beaded along his helmet rim are bronze.
The words on his page are bronze. Their meaning bronze.

Sunk in his bronze world he stands, enchanted.
His bronze mind is deep among the dead.
Sunk so deep among the dead that, much
As he would like to remember us all, he cannot.

Ted Hughes (1930 –   )

LANGUAGE OF POETRY

Simile – a direct comparison of one thing with another, often using the word 'like' or 'as'

e.g. as light/And straight as a dove's flight.

Metaphor – a comparison of two separate things which leaves out the word 'like' or 'as', so the poet seems to be saying one thing actually is something else

e.g. cradle of a journey

Extended metaphor – sometimes a single metaphor can run throughout a poem from beginning to end. See the poem on p.16 for an example of an 'extended' metaphor.

Personification – a metaphor which talks about a thing as if it were a person. The statue of the soldier is spoken of in this poem as if it were a living person

e.g. His bronze mind is deep among the dead.

[continued over...]

- Poetry is meant to be read aloud. Practice reading 'Platform One' aloud. Think about the tone of your voice, the pace (or speed) of your reading and which words need emphasising. Try reading lines and phrases in different ways. Which style or tone conveys the sense of the poem better?

- The 'Cornish Riviera' refers to holidays by train to the seasides of Cornwall. How does Ted Hughes convey the excitement of going on holiday?

- By comparison, the statue is very still. How are we told this? Look closely at the language and make notes about the words the poet has chosen.

- Identify the similes, metaphors and personification in this poem. What effect do these have in the poem and on you personally?

- Write a few paragraphs explaining your thoughts and feelings about this poem. You should aim to explain how your response to the poem has developed with successive readings. Follow this sequence in your writing:

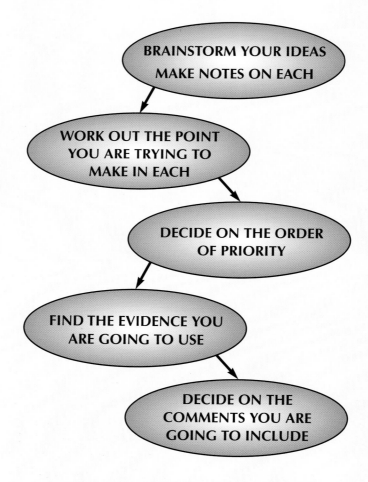

BRAINSTORM YOUR IDEAS
MAKE NOTES ON EACH

WORK OUT THE POINT YOU ARE TRYING TO MAKE IN EACH

DECIDE ON THE ORDER OF PRIORITY

FIND THE EVIDENCE YOU ARE GOING TO USE

DECIDE ON THE COMMENTS YOU ARE GOING TO INCLUDE

Now you are ready to do your writing.

The next poem, by Robert Southey, was written in 1798 but it looks back to 1704 when the Duke of Marlborough defeated the French and Austrians in the Napoleonic Wars. It has been divided into three segments. Read each segment aloud, then carry out the task before moving on.

THE BATTLE OF BLENHEIM

I
It was a summer evening,
    Old Kaspar's work was done,
And he before his cottage door
    Was sitting in the sun,
And by him sported on the green
His little grandchild Wilhelmine.

II
She saw her brother Peterkin
    Roll something large and round,
Which he beside the rivulet
    In playing there had found;
He came to ask what he had found,
That was so large, and smooth, and round.

III
Old Kaspar took it from the boy,
    Who stood expectant by;
And then the old man shook his head,
    And, with a natural sigh,
'Tis some poor fellow's skull,' said he,
'Who fell in the great victory.

IV
'I find them in the garden,
    For there's many here about;
And often when I go to plough,
    The ploughshare turns them out!
For many thousand men,' said he,
    'Were slain in that great victory.'

V
'Now tell us what 'twas all about,'
    Young Peterkin, he cries;
And little Wilhelmine looks up
    With wonder-waiting eyes;
'Now tell us all about the war,
    And what they fought each other for.'

The first three verses set the scene. Explain in your own words what that scene is. Include details about the atmosphere of this family gathering. How is the subject of war brought into this and does this change the atmosphere?

VI
'It was the English,' Kaspar cried,
    'Who put the French to rout;
But what they fought each other for,
    I could not make well out;
But everybody said,' quoth he,
'That 'twas a famous victory.

VII
'My father lived in Blenheim then,
    Yon little stream hard by;
They burnt his dwelling to the ground,
    And he was forced to fly;
So with his wife and child he fled,
Nor had he where to rest his head.

[continued over...]

Verses IV to IX tell us about the details of the fighting. What specific details are you given? Did Old Kaspar witness these events himself? How do you know this?

VIII

'With fire and sword the country round
  Was wasted far and wide,
And many a childing mother then,
  And new-born baby died;
But things like that, you know, must be
At every famous victory.

IX

'They say it was a shocking sight
  After the field was won;
For many thousand bodies here
  Lay rotting in the sun;
But things like that, you know, must be
After a famous victory.

X

'Great praise the Duke of Marlbro' won,
  And our good Prince Eugene.'
'Why 'twas a very wicked thing!'
  Said little Wilhelmine.
'Nay... nay... my little girl,' quoth he,
'It was a famous victory.'

XI

'And everybody praised the Duke
  Who this great fight did win.'
'But what good came of it at last?'
  Quoth little Peterkin.
'Why that I cannot tell,' said he
'But 'twas a famous victory.'

Robert Southey (1774–1843)

• What is Old Kaspar's feeling about this battle? Do the children agree with him? What does the poem tell you about people's attitudes to victory?

• This appears to be quite a simple poem – but is it? Much of the poem is written as speech. What effect does this have on you

  a) when you look at the poem

  b) when you hear the poem read aloud?

• In pairs work out the rhyme scheme of this poem. Is the rhyme scheme regular throughout the poem?

• Did you notice the rhymes when you were reading it aloud? Do you notice them when you look at the poem on the page? Why do you think it was written using rhyme?

• Write a drama script for a scene between Wilhelmine and Peterkin which takes place immediately after the end of the poem.

LANGUAGE OF POETRY

Rhyme – most people can recognise rhyming words. Rhyming words can add considerably to the sound and pattern of a poem. There are different ways of using rhyme. In this poem it is end-rhyme.

e.g. He came to ask what he had found,
That was so large, and smooth, and round.

Rhyme-scheme is usually represented by ABCD to show the order of the end-rhymes.

It was a summer evening,	A
Old Kaspar's work was done,	B
And he before his cottage door	C
Was sitting in the sun,	B
And by him sported on the green	D
His little grandchild Wilhelmine	D

Another form of rhyme, not evident here, is **internal rhyme**. This is when the rhymes come in the middle of lines rather than at the end. Look out for examples of this form of rhyme as you read the rest of the poems in this book.

SAND

We have seen sand frothing like the sea
About our wheels, and in our wake
Clouds rolling yellow and opaque,
Thick-smoking from the ground;
Wrapped in the dust from sun and sky
Without a mark to guide them by
Men drove alone unseeing in the cloud,
Peering to find a track, to find a way,
With eyes stung red, clown-faces coated grey.
Then with sore lips we cursed the sand,
Cursed this sullen gritty land
– Cursed and dragged on our blind and clogging way.

We have felt the fevered Khamsin* blow
Which whips the desert into sting and spite
Of dry-sand driving rain (the only rain
The parched and dusty sand-lands know.
The hot dry driven sand): the desert floor
Whipped by the wind drives needles in the air
Which pricked our eyelids blind; and in a night,
Sifting the drifted sandhill grain by grain,
Covers our shallow tracks, our laboured road,
Makes false the maps we made with such slow care.

And we have seen wonders, spinning towers of sand
– Moving pillars of cloud by day –
Which passed and twitched our tents away;
Lakes where no water was, and in the sky
Grey shimmering palms. We have learned the sun and stars
And new simplicities, living by our cars
In wastes without one tree or living thing,
Where the flat horizon's level ring
Is equal everywhere without a change.

Yet sand has been kind for us to lie at ease,
Its soft-dug walls have sheltered and made a shield
From fear and danger, and the chilly night.
And as we quit this bare unlovely land,
Strangely again see houses, hills, and trees,
We will remember older things than these,
Indigo skies pricked out with brilliant light,
The smooth unshadowed candour of the sand.

John Jarmain

* Khamsin – a wind that blows from the Sahara,
whipping up stinging sand storms.

[continued over...]

- Design a storyboard (see the Help box below) for the poem 'Sand' to show: the narrative; the landscape; the actions of the soldiers; the characters' thoughts and reactions.

Use between five and twelve storyboard frames. Next to your drawings write quotations from the poem which help to explain what you have chosen to show. You may need more than one quotation and these may come from different parts of the poem. Set your work out like this:

'sand frothing like the sea about our wheels'

'Clouds rolling yellow and opaque'

'Men drove alone unseeing in the cloud
Peering to find a track'

'Wrapped in the dust from sun and sky
Without a mark to guide them by'

- Use the library to research the background to this poem:

Use your information to devise a role-play based on the characters and situation represented in the poem 'Sand' where you show you can imagine and explore the ideas in the poem,

or

Discuss what life as a soldier fighting in the North African desert might have been like, based on your research and understanding of the poem 'Sand',

or

Write a description of the landscape and sounds of the desert based on your exploration of this poet's experience.

HELP

A storyboard is a media technique to show, by sketching in a frame to represent a camera shot, what would be seen on the TV or film screen.

Along with these sketches, a storyboard notes the sound and camera techniques required for each shot.

John Jarmain was killed in the Western Desert, North Africa, in 1942.

RETURNING, WE HEAR THE LARKS

Sombre the night is.
And though we have our lives, we know
What sinister threat lurks there.

Dragging these anguished limbs, we only know
This poison-blasted track opens on our camp –
On a little safe sleep.

But hark! joy – joy – strange joy.
Lo! heights of night ringing with unseen larks.
Music showering our upturned list'ning faces.

Death could drop from the dark
As easily as song –
But song only dropped,
Like a blind man's dreams on the sand
By dangerous tides;
Like a girl's dark hair for she dreams no ruin lies there,
Or her kisses where a serpent hides.

Isaac Rosenberg (1890–1918)

HELP

When writing a coursework piece you should try to write in the following way:

POINT to be made

EVIDENCE to be used

COMMENTARY to explain or justify it

Your notes should supply most of the POINTS you will need to include. Now go back to the poems and select the EVIDENCE (quotations) you will use to support the points you make.

- Read this poem several times. Each stanza is appealing to one or more of our senses. Try to identify these. Which words or phrases helped you to decide?

- Write two paragraphs explaining

  - how the poet felt before he heard the lark.

  - what the lark's music made him feel and think.

- Remind yourself of the two poems 'Sand' and 'Returning, We Hear the Larks'.
  Both poems suggest that beauty can be found even when at war and in danger.
  Compare these two poems and make notes on the following points:

SAND		RETURNING...
	What is the danger involved?	
	How is this danger conveyed to the reader?	
	What does the poet find beautiful?	
	What feelings are expressed about the beauty?	
	What tone is there to the poem?	
	Which poem seems more effective to you?	

- Using your notes, and the quotations you have selected as evidence, plan, draft and write an essay based on the following title (refer to the Help box above for further guidance):

  Compare and contrast the ideas of danger and beauty in the two poems, 'Sand' and 'Returning, We Hear the Larks'. How does each poet convey these to his reader?

Isaac Rosenberg enlisted as a private in 1915 and served in France. He was killed in action in April 1918 and buried in a mass grave.

The following poem was written by Rudyard Kipling when he was a reporter in
South Africa during the Boer War (1899–1902). The hyaena is a bush scavenger. Here
Kipling describes how the hyaenas would dig up freshly buried soldiers for food.

THE HYAENAS

After the burial-parties leave
  And the baffled kites have fled;
The wise hyaenas come out at eve
  To take account of our dead.

How he died and why he died
  Troubles them not a whit.
They snout the bushes and stones aside
  And dig till they come to it.

They only resolute they shall eat
  That they and their mates may thrive,
And they know the dead are safer meat
  Than the weakest thing alive.

(For a goat may butt, and a worm may sting,
  And a child will sometimes stand;
But a poor dead soldier of the king
  Can never lift a hand.)

They whoop and halloo and scatter the dirt
  Until their tushes white
Take good hold in the army shirt,
  And tug the corpse to light,

And the pitiful face is shewn again
  For an instant ere they close;
But it is not discovered to living men –
  Only to God and those

Who, being soulless, are free from shame,
  Whatever meat they may find.
Nor do they defile the dead man's name –
  That is reserved for his kind.

Rudyard Kipling (1865–1936)

- Which words and phrases
  express the poet's sense of horror?

- Which words show his understanding of the
  actions of the hyaenas?

- In what way is man shown to be worse than
  these hyaenas?

Philip Johnstone imagines how the soldiers who lost their lives might later be remembered. 'High Wood' was written in 1918 and anticipated the conducted tours of the battlefields which became popular after the First World War.

HIGH WOOD

Ladies and gentlemen, this is High Wood,
Called by the French, Bois des Fourneaux,
The famous spot which in Nineteen-Sixteen,
July, August and September was the scene
Of long and bitterly contested strife,
By reason of its High commanding site.
Observe the effect of shell-fire in the trees
Standing and fallen; here is wire; this trench
For months inhabited, twelve times changed hands;
(They soon fall in), used later as a grave.
It has been said on good authority
That in the fighting for this patch of wood
Were killed somewhere above eight thousand men,
Of whom the greater part were buried here,
This mound on which you stand being...
                                    Madame, please,
You are requested kindly not to touch
Or take away the Company's property
As souvenirs; you'll find we have on sale
A large variety, all guaranteed.
As I was saying, all is as it was,
This is an unknown British officer,
The tunic having lately rotted off.
Please follow me – this way...
                            the *path*, sir, *please*,
The ground which was secured at great expense
The Company keeps absolutely untouched,
And in that dug-out (genuine) we provide
Refreshments at a reasonable rate.
You are requested not to leave about
Paper, or ginger-beer bottles, or orange-peel,
There are waste-paper baskets at the gate.

Philip Johnstone

- Read this poem aloud, twice.

The run-on lines (enjambement) make it sound like everyday speech. Identify the other parts of the poem that seem more like prose.

- Discuss with a partner what you expect a poem to be like. Make a list of the different aspects of writing which you consider to be 'poetry'. Can you spot these aspects in the poem 'High Wood'?

HELP

In examinations you have to write an answer to a question or task in an allocated time. The following exercise is practice in the skills of planning and writing in a limited time, making sure that you write a complete answer which contains all the points you wish to make.

- You have 20 minutes to answer the following question:

In what ways are the hyaenas and the tour guide similar in the poems 'The Hyaenas' and 'High Wood'? Refer to each poem in detail.

In pairs or small groups, work on the following poem and prepare it in readiness to perform to camera or a live audience. The aim of your performance is to convey the meaning and, more importantly, the feeling in the poem to your audience. The tone (sound) of a poem is very important and helps you to understand its meaning. You need to have a good understanding of the poem's meaning in order to perform it.

- Prepare the poem as follows. Read it through carefully twice, discuss and make notes on

  - the meanings of words you are unfamiliar with

  - what tone you will need to have for different sections of the poem

  - which words you are going to emphasise

  - how you are going to use pauses and the overall pace of the poem

  - who is going to say what.

The notes you make will help you to write about the poem later.

DRUMMER HODGE

They throw in Drummer Hodge, to rest
  Uncoffined – just as found:
His landmark is a kopje-crest[1]
  That breaks the veldt[2] around;
And foreign constellations west
  Each night above his mound.

Young Hodge the Drummer never knew –
  Fresh from his Wessex home –
The meaning of the broad Karoo[3],
  The Bush, the dusty loam,
And why uprose to nightly view
  Strange stars amid the gloam[4].

Yet portion of that unknown plain
  Will Hodge for ever be;
His homely Northern breast and brain
  Grow to some Southern tree,
And strange-eyed constellations reign
  His stars eternally.

Thomas Hardy (1840–1928)

Thomas Hardy

[1]small hill [2]open grassland [3]dry uplands [4]evening

Thomas Hardy was already well known for his novels when he wrote about the Boer War in South Africa. This poem was inspired by a local Wessex drummer boy whose death in the war was reported in a Dorset newspaper. 'Hodge' was a nick-name usually given to country lads. Hardy includes several South African words as a way of showing how unfamiliar the country was to the boy and to his readers.

THE SOLDIER

If I should die, think only this of me:
   That there's some corner of a foreign field
That is for ever England. There shall be
   In that rich earth a richer dust concealed;
A dust whom England bore, shaped, made aware,
   Gave, once, her flowers to love, her ways to roam,
A body of England's, breathing English air,
   Washed by the rivers, blest by suns of home.

And think, this heart, all evil shed away,
   A pulse in the eternal mind, no less
Gives something back the thoughts by England given;
    Her sights and sounds; dreams happy as her day;
And laughter, learnt of friends; and gentleness,
   In hearts at peace, under an English heaven.

                      Rupert Brooke (1887–1915)

Rupert Brooke saw little action during the First World War. He was unaware of the conditions in the trenches and at the front which so motivated poets such as Wilfred Owen, Isaac Rosenberg and Siegfried Sassoon. He died of blood poisoning in the Aegean in April 1915.

LANGUAGE OF POETRY

A **sonnet** is a poem which has a strict verse form of fourteen lines with a set rhyme pattern. The most common rhyme schemes are:

ABBA ABBA CDE CDE

ABAB CDCD EFEF GG

Traditionally, sonnets were written in lines containing ten syllables with an unstressed syllable followed by a stressed one (called **iambic pentameter**).

For example:

   If I should die, think only this of me:
      That there's some corner of a foreign field...

The first eight lines of a sonnet are called the **octave**, the last six lines are called the **sestet**.

- The poem 'The Soldier' is an example of a sonnet. What is the rhyme scheme?

- Write a summary of what the poet is saying in this poem. Select five words or phrases which best convey his feelings. Explain your selection and understanding of these to a partner.

George Gordon Byron (1788–1824) became Lord Byron when he was ten years old. He travelled abroad extensively before eventually leaving England for good in 1816. Sennacherib, King of Assyria from 709BC to his death in 681BC, destroyed a series of Judaean cities and besieged Jerusalem. According to the Bible, Sennacherib's defeat was due to an angel of the Lord intervening on the city's behalf. This historical conflict is the subject of the following poem by Byron.

THE DESTRUCTION OF SENNACHERIB

The Assyrian came down like the wolf on the fold,
And his cohorts were gleaming in purple and gold;
And the sheen of their spears was like stars on the sea,
When the blue wave rolls nightly on deep Galilee.

Like the leaves of the forest when Summer is green,
That host with their banners at sunset were seen:
Like the leaves of the forest when Autumn hath blown,
That host on the morrow lay wither'd and strown.

For the Angel of Death spread his wings on the blast,
And breathed in the face of the foe as he pass'd;
And the eyes of the sleepers wax'd deadly and chill,
And their hearts but once heaved, and for ever grew still!

And there lay the steed with his nostril all wide,
But through it there roll'd not the breath of his pride;
And the foam of his gasping lay white on the turf,
And cold as the spray of the rock-beating surf.

And there lay the rider distorted and pale,
With the dew on his brow, and the rust on his mail;
And the tents were all silent, the banners alone,
The lances uplifted, the trumpet unblown.

And the widows of Ashur are loud in their wail,
And the idols are broken in the temple of Baal;
And the might of the Gentile, unsmote by the sword,
Hath melted like snow in the glance of the Lord!

Lord Byron (1788–1824)

> *Isaiah Ch 36, verses 33–37*
>
> 'Therefore thus says the LORD concerning the King of Assyria; He shall not come into this city, or shoot an arrow there, or come before it with a shield, or cast up a siege mound against it. By the way that he came, by the same he shall return, and he shall not come into this city, says the LORD. For I will defend this city to save it, for my own sake and for the sake of my servant David.'
> And the Angel of the LORD went forth, and slew a hundred and eighty-five thousand in the camp of the Assyrians; and when men arose early in the morning, behold, these were all dead bodies. Then Sennach'erib King of Assyria departed, and went home and dwelt at Nin'eveh.'

- The poem contains an **extended metaphor** (see page 5). What is it?

- What does the 'Angel of Death' actually do in this poem?

- Compare the biblical account with that in the poem. How are they different?

- Presumably the inhabitants of the city were pleased at the way the battle turned out. Imagine that you were in the city, write about these events from the victor's point of view.

The next two poems describe less happy memories of war. The Duke of Wellington said, 'Nothing except a battle lost can be half so melancholy as a battle won.' Siegfried Sassoon (1886–1967) fought in the First World War and arrived at the front in November 1915. Up until that time his poetry was generally supportive of the Great War. At the front he demonstrated remarkable courage and won the Military Cross for bringing back wounded men from no-man's land and capturing a trench full of German soldiers. In 1916 he was invalided home and turned his anger about the war against the military commanders, politicians and an uncaring public. By reading 'Does it Matter?' you will be able to work out why.

DOES IT MATTER?

Does it matter? – losing your legs?...
For people will always be kind,
And you need not show that you mind
When the others come in after hunting
To gobble their muffins and eggs.

Does it matter? – losing your sight?...
'There's such splendid work for the blind;'
And people will always be kind,
As you sit on the terrace remembering
And turning your face to the light.

Do they matter? – those dreams from the pit?...
You can drink and forget and be glad,
And people won't say that you're mad,
For they know you've fought for your country
And no one will worry a bit.

                 Siegfried Sassoon (1886–1967)

Siegfried Sassoon

- How would you read this poem aloud to bring out the real meaning behind the words?

- What feelings did the poet want you to have about his questions?

- Write your own reply to the question in this poem. This could be in poetic form or in prose. In your planning, select the comments in 'Does it Matter?' that you consider are important to respond to.

LANGUAGE OF POETRY

Irony means saying one thing when really you mean another and is a method which can be used by poets to achieve a deeper meaning.

Irony can be used as a subtle way of mocking someone or their views. Understatement and concealment can often convey a point of view more powerfully than direct statement.

Wilfred Owen (1893–1918) is probably the best known First World War poet.
Early in 1917 he was in the front line at the Somme and his letters to his mother
reveal the sheer horror of the war at the front in winter. He was invalided in
1917 at the same time as Sassoon who encouraged his writing. Owen insisted on
being sent back to the front in 1918 and died there a week before Armistice. His
poem 'Dulce et Decorum est' is the most famous war poem for GCSE students.
In 'Disabled' Owen contemplates life as a severely disabled soldier.

DISABLED

He sat in a wheeled chair, waiting for dark,
And shivered in his ghastly suit of grey,
Legless, sewn short at elbow. Through the park
Voices of boys rang saddening like a hymn,
Voices of play and pleasure after day,
Till gathering sleep had mothered them from him.

About this time Town used to swing so gay
When glow-lamps budded in the light blue trees,
And girls glanced lovelier as the air grew dim, –
In the old times, before he threw away his knees.
Now he will never feel again how slim
Girls' waists are, or how warm their subtle hands;
All of them touch him like some queer disease.

There was an artist silly for his face,
For it was younger than his youth, last year.
Now, he is old; his back will never brace;
He's lost his colour very far from here,
Poured it down shell-holes till the veins ran dry,
And half his lifetime lapsed in the hot race,
And leap of purple spurted from his thigh.

One time he'd liked a blood-smear down his leg,
After the matches, carried shoulder-high.
It was after football, when he'd drunk a peg.
He'd thought he'd better join. – He wonders why.
Someone had said he'd look a god in kilts,
That's why; and may be, too, to please his Meg;
Aye, that was it, to please the giddy jilts
He asked to join. He didn't have to beg;
Smiling they wrote his lie; aged nineteen years.
Germans he scarcely thought of, all their guilt,
And Austria's, did not move him. And no fears
Of Fear came yet. He thought of jewelled hilts
For daggers in plaid socks; of smart salutes;
And care for arms; and leave; and pay arrears;
Esprit de corps*; and hints for young recruits.
And soon he was drafted out with drums and cheers.

Some cheered him home, but not as crowds cheer Goal.
Only a solemn man who brought him fruits
Thanked him; and then inquired about his soul.

Now, he will spend a few sick years in Institutes,
And do what things the rules consider wise,
And take whatever pity they may dole.
To-night he noticed how the women's eyes
Passed from him to the strong men that were whole.
How cold and late it is! Why don't they come
And put him into bed? Why don't they come?

Wilfred Owen (1893–1918)

*esprit de corps – means loyalty to one's comrades.

In 'Disabled' Wilfred Owen imagines the thoughts and feelings of a young soldier who has lost all of his limbs and has to rely on other people to do everything for him. The first and the last stanza are about him now; the rest of the poem thinks back to his life before he was wounded.

- Make a list of all the things he used to do and the things he enjoyed.

- Do the same for the things he is able to do now and the way he feels.

- Write a summary of his reasons for joining up.

- How does the poem make you feel about the soldier? Select the words and phrases which work on your feelings.

- What does the future hold for this person? What might he mean by 'waiting for dark'? Write a paragraph describing his thoughts as he waits for the nurse to appear.

- Look again at 'Does it Matter?' The subject of each poem is essentially the same but the style of writing is very different.

  Working in pairs, make notes about the style of these two poems. Consider the following:

  – vocabulary used – and how you respond to it

  – images which come to mind

  – structure of the poem – including rhyme scheme

  – use of the past and present

  – tone.

  Explore your ideas with those of another pair.

- Imagine you are Meg. How do you feel about your lover now? Do you intend staying with him or do you no longer feel anything for him? Write a letter to your wounded lover. Consider carefully what you might say to him about the past and the present as well as the future.

ANTHEM FOR DOOMED YOUTH

What passing bells for these who die as cattle?
   – Only the monstrous anger of the guns.
  Only the stuttering rifles' rapid rattle
Can patter out their hasty orisons.
No mockeries now for them; no prayers nor bells;
  Nor any voice of mourning save the choirs,–
The shrill demented choirs of wailing shells;
  And bugles calling for them from sad shires.

What candles may be held to speed them all?
  Not in the hands of boys but in their eyes
Shall shine the holy glimmers of good-byes.
  The pallor of girls' brows shall be their pall;
Their flowers the tenderness of patient minds,
And each slow dusk a drawing-down of blinds.

Wilfred Owen

Wilfred Owen

In this sonnet Owen voices his opinion about the young soldiers, many of them still in their teens, who are slaughtered in battle. Wilfred Owen wrote several drafts of the poem before the final version you see above. On the page opposite are the first and third drafts of the poem. Read them carefully and then complete the tasks below.

- Individual words are very important in order to convey exactly the right message to the reader. What ideas and feelings are conveyed by the word 'dead' compared with the word 'doomed' in the title of this poem?

- Look carefully at the octave of each draft, (look back to page 15 for details about the sonnet form). Make a list of the changes Owen made. What effect do these changes have?

- What do you usually associate with an anthem? Why do you think Owen wanted to call this poem an anthem?

- There are many religious references in 'Anthem for Doomed Youth'. Work out which words or phrases have some religious connotations. What do they add to the message of the poem?

- Discuss in pairs the different ideas and feelings in the octave and the sestet of the final version of this sonnet (above).

- Look again at 'The Soldier' on page 15. Both these poems are sonnets. How does the sonnet form add to the impact of the lament in each poem? Which, to you, is the more forceful poem?

First draft

Anthem for Dead Youth.

What passing bells for these who die so fast?
— Only the monstrous anger of our guns.
Let the majestic insults of their mouths
Be as the requiem of their burials.
Of choristers and holy music, none;
Nor any voice of mourning, save the wail
The long drawn wail of high far sailing shells.

What candles may we hold for those lost souls?
— Not in the hands of boys, but in their eyes
Shall many candles shine, and
And women's wide spreaded arms shall be their wreaths,
And pallor of girls cheeks shall be their palls.
Their flowers, the tenderness of minds.
And each slow dusk, a drawing down of blinds.

First Draft
(With Sassoon's amendments.)

Anthem for Dead Youth.

What passing-bells for you who die in herds?
— Only the monstrous anger of the guns!
— Only the stuttering rifles' rattled words
Can patter out your hasty orisons.
No chants for you, nor balms, nor wreaths, nor bells,
Nor any voice of mourning, save the choirs,
The shrill demented choirs of wailing shells;
And bugles calling for you from sad shires.

What candles may we hold to speed you all?
Not in the hands of boys, but in their eyes
Shall shine the holy lights of long goodbyes.
The pallor of girls' brows shall be your pall;
Your flower, the tenderness of mortal minds,
And each slow dusk, a drawing down of blinds.

Wilfred Owen.

Third draft

SPRING OFFENSIVE

Halted against the shade of a last hill,
They fed, and lying easy, were at ease
And, finding comfortable chests and knees,
Carelessly slept. But many there stood still
To face the stark blank sky beyond the ridge,
Knowing their feet had come to the end of the
world.

Marvelling they stood, and watched the long grass
swirled
By the May breeze, murmurous with wasp and
midge,
For though the summer oozed into their veins
Like an injected drug for their bodies' pains,
Sharp on their souls hung the imminent line of
grass,
Fearfully flashed the sky's mysterious glass.

Hour after hour they ponder the warm field, –
And the far valley behind, where the buttercup
Had blessed with gold their slow boots coming up,
Where even the little brambles would not yield,
But clutched and clung to them like sorrowing
hands.
They breathe like trees unstirred.

Till like a cold gust thrills the little word
At which each body and its soul begird
And tighten them for battle. No alarms
Of bugles, no high flags, no clamorous haste, –
Only a lift and flare of eyes that faced
The sun, like a friend with whom their love is
done.
O larger shone that smile against the sun, –
Mightier than His whose bounty these have
spurned.

So, soon they topped the hill, and raced together
Over an open stretch of herb and heather
Exposed. And instantly the whole sky burned
With fury against them; earth set sudden cups
In thousands for their blood; and the green slope
Chasmed and steepened sheer to infinite space.

Of them who running on that last high place
Leapt to swift unseen bullets, or went up
On the hot blast and fury of hell's upsurge,
Or plunged and fell away past this world's verge,
Some say God caught them even before they fell.

But what say such as from existence's brink
Ventured but drave too swift to sink,
The few who rushed in the body to enter hell,
And there out-fiending all its fiends and flames
With superhuman inhumanities,
Long-famous glories, immemorial shames –
And crawling slowly back, have by degrees
Regained cool peaceful air in wonder –
Why speak not they of comrades that went under?

Wilfred Owen

- In pairs work through this poem stanza by stanza. Explain what happens in each as well as the mood. These words may help you:

SAVAGE   RELUCTANT   RELAXED
SHARP   HEALING   EXCITING
PENSIVE

- The vocabulary in this poem has been selected very carefully. Not only does the poem tell a story but it also creates an atmosphere. Select words or phrases to put in these boxes –

ACTION	ATMOSPHERE
halted	were at ease
fed	stark, blank sky

- Select five powerful images from the poem and sketch them. Use one line from the poem as a caption for each sketch.

- Not all the soldiers reacted in the same way. What are the different behaviours? Why might these soldiers react differently?

Edmund Blunden (1896–1974), poet and writer, fought in France during the First World War, experienced the ghastly carnage of the Battle of the Somme in 1916, and survived to write vividly of his experiences. *Undertones of War* was first published in 1928. Here is an extract from it.

ARRIVING AT THE FRONT

'It was now approaching the beginning of November, and the days were melancholy and the colour of clay. We took over that deathtrap known as the Schwaben Redoubt, the way to which lay through the fallen fortress of Thiepval. One had heard the worst accounts of the place, and they were true. Crossing the Ancre again at Black Horse Bridge, one went up through the scanty skeleton houses of Authuille, and climbing the dirty little road over the steep bank, one immediately entered the land of despair. Bodies, bodies and their useless gear heaped the gross waste ground; the slimy road was soon only a mud track which passed a whitish tumulus of ruin with lurking entrances, some spikes that had been pine trees, a bricked cellar or two, and died out. The village pond, so blue on the map, had completely disappeared. The Ligne de Pommiers had been grubbed up. The shell-holes were mostly small lakes of what was merely rusty water, but had a red and foul semblance of blood. Paths glistened weakly from tenable point to point. Of the dead, one was conspicuous. He was a Scottish soldier, and was kneeling, facing east, so that one could scarcely credit death in him; he was seen at some little distance from the usual tracks, and no-one had much time in Thiepval just then for sight-seeing or burying. Death could not kneel so, I thought, and approaching I ascertained with a sudden shrivelling of spirit that Death could and did.

Beyond the area called Thiepval on the map a trench called St. Martin's Lane led forward; unhappy he who got into it! It was blasted by intense bombardment into a broad shapeless gorge, and pools of mortar-like mud filled most of it. A few duckboards lay half submerged along the parapet, and these were perforce used by our companies, and calculatingly and fiercely shelled at moments by the enemy. The wooden track ended, and the men fought their way on through the gluey morass, until not one or two were reduced to tears and impotent wild cries to God. They were not yet at the worst of their duty, for the Schwaben Redoubt ahead was an almost obliterated cocoon of trenches in which mud, and death, and life were much the same thing – and there the deep dugouts, which faced the German guns, were cancerous with torn bodies, and to pass an entrance was to gulp poison; in one place a corpse had apparently been thrust in to stop up a doorway's dangerous displacement, and an arm swung stupidly. Men of the next battalion were found in mud up to the armpits, and their fate was not spoken of; those who found them could not get them out. The whole zone was a corpse, and the mud itself mortified.'

- Copy the following table and complete it using details from the writing only.

the weather	the shell-holes	the men	the area
days were melancholy	small lakes	a Scottish soldier	deathtrap

- Use these details to write your own poem. You could start by writing one stanza on each of these four aspects. Select the words you use with great care in order to create the right atmosphere and tone. You will probably have to re-draft your poem. Look back at the drafts of 'Anthem for Doomed Youth' for some ideas about the changes you could make.

- Work with a partner to improve your poem. Read it aloud and listen to their comments about structure and tone.

Vernon Scannell, in this poem, looks back on his service during the Second
World War. He imagines a moment of peace.

ROUTE MARCH REST

They marched in staggered columns through the lanes
Drowsy with dust and summer, rifles slung.
All other-ranks wore helmets and the sun
Drummed on bobbing metal plates and purred
Inside their skulls; the thumping tramp of boots
On gravel crunched. B company had become
A long machine that clanked and throbbed. The reek
Of leather, sweat and rifle-oil was thick
And khaki on the body of the day.
All dainty fragrances were shouldered out
Though thrush and blackbird song could not be stilled
And teased some favoured regions of the air.

They reached a village and the order came
To halt and fall out for a rest. The men
Unslung their rifles, lit up cigarettes,
And sprawled or squatted on the village green.
Opposite the green, next to the church,
The school, whose open windows with wild flowers
In glass jars on the sills framed pools of dark,
Was silent, cool; but from the playground sprayed
The calls of children, bright as buttercups,
Until a handbell called them in from play
And then B company was ordered back
To fall in on the road in their platoons
And start the march again.
                      Beyond the church
They passed the marble plinth and saw the roll
Of names, too many surely for this small
Community, and as the files trudged on,
Faintly from the school, like breaths of flowers
But half-remembered, children's voices rose:
'All things bright and beautiful,' they sang,
Frail sound, already fading, soon to die.

Vernon Scannell (1922–)

- Complete the following:

  I think this poem is about...

I think the best phrases/lines are...
because...

I think the poem was written because...

I think the weakest part of the poem is...
because...

- In small groups discuss your individual
  answers and compare your selection.
  Explain in detail the reason for your
  comments and be prepared to persuade
  others.

- On your own, write up your answer in
  four paragraphs in a time set for you by
  your teacher. Remember to use quotes
  from the poem to support your
  comments.

Edward Thomas was born in London in 1878. He wrote only a few war poems, his main inspiration being the Gloucestershire countryside – a love which is clearly evident even in his war poetry. He was killed in action in Arras on 9th April 1917.

AS THE TEAM'S HEAD BRASS

As the team's head brass flashed out on the turn
The lovers disappeared into the wood.
I sat among the boughs of the fallen elm
That strewed the angle of the fallow, and
Watched the plough narrowing a yellow square
Of charlock. Every time the horses turned
Instead of treading me down, the ploughman leaned
Upon the handles to say or ask a word,
About the weather, next about the war.
Scraping the share he faced towards the wood,
And screwed along the furrow until the brass flashed
Once more.

        The blizzard felled the elm whose crest
I sat in, by a woodpecker's round hole,
The ploughman said, 'When will they take it away?'
'When the war's over.' So the talk began –
One minute and an interval of ten,
A minute more and the same interval.
'Have you been out?' 'No.' 'And don't want to, perhaps?'
'If I could spare an arm. I shouldn't want to lose
A leg. If I should lose my head, why, so,
If I should want nothing more... Have many gone
From here?' 'Yes.' 'Many lost?' 'Yes, a good few.
Only two teams work on the farm this year.
One of my mates is dead. The second day
In France they killed him. It was back in March,
The very night of the blizzard, too. Now if
He had stayed here we should have moved the tree.'
'And I should not have sat here. Everything
Would have been different. For it would have been
Another world.' 'Ay, and a better, though
If we could see all all might seem good.' Then
The lovers came out of the wood again:
The horses started and for the last time
I watched the clods crumble and topple over
After the ploughshare and the stumbling team.

                    Edward Thomas (1878–1917)

FIFTY FAGGOTS

There they stand, on their ends, the fifty faggots
That once were underwood of hazel and ash
In Jenny Pink's Copse. Now, by the hedge
Close packed, they make a thicket fancy alone
Can creep through with the mouse and the wren. Next Spring
A blackbird or a robin will nest there,
Accustomed to them, thinking they will remain
Whatever is for ever to a bird:
This Spring it is too late; the swift has come.
'Twas a hot day for carrying them up:
Better they will never warm me, though they must
Light several Winter's fires. Before they are done
The war will have ended, many other things
Have ended, maybe, that I can no more
Foresee or more control than robin or wren.

Edward Thomas (1878–1917)

- Reflect on how these poems are different to the poems by war poets that you have read so far.

- Read through 'As the Team's Head Brass' again and work out who says what. What effect does the narrator's voice have on the reader? Discuss with a partner the attitude to war of those who stayed behind.

- The progress of time and its effect on events are important themes in Edward Thomas's poetry. How are these themes treated in 'As the Team's Head Brass' and 'Fifty Faggots'? How has the war influenced the course of events in each poem?

- 'Edward Thomas loved nature'. Support this statement, using the poems 'As the Team's Head Brass' and 'Fifty Faggots'.

or

Compare the war poetry of Edward Thomas with that of Wilfred Owen.

The next poem, by Thomas Hardy, imagines a lonely woman waiting for news of her husband far away, fighting in the Boer War in South Africa (the 'far South Land').

A WIFE IN LONDON

I
She sits in the tawny vapour
  That the Thames-side lanes have uprolled,
  Behind whose webby fold on fold
Like a waning taper
  The street-lamp glimmers cold.

A messenger's knock cracks smartly,
  Flashed news is in her hand
  Of meaning it dazes to understand
Though shaped so shortly:
  He – has fallen – in the far South Land...

II
'Tis the morrow; the fog hangs thicker,
  The postman nears and goes:
  A letter is brought whose lines disclose
By the firelight flicker
  His hand, whom the worm now knows:

III
Fresh – firm – penned in highest feather –
  Page-full of his hoped return,
  And of home planned jaunts by brake and burn
In the summer weather,
  And of new love that they would learn.

Thomas Hardy (1840–1928)

Walt Whitman worked as a wound dresser in rather basic camp hospitals during the American Civil War (1861–5). During this time he witnessed many soldiers suffering and dying. In the poem on the next page he imagines the family of one casualty receiving the news at home.

[continued over...]

COME UP FROM THE FIELDS FATHER

Come up from the fields father, here's a letter from our Pete,
And come to the front door mother, here's a letter from thy dear son.

Lo, 'tis autumn,
Lo, where the trees, deeper green, yellower and redder,
Cool and sweeten Ohio's villages with leaves fluttering in the moderate wind,

Where apples ripe in the orchards hang and grapes on the trellis'd vines,
(Smell you the smell of the grapes on the vines?
Smell you the buckwheat where the bees were lately buzzing?)
Above all, lo, the sky so calm, so transparent after the rain, and with wondrous clouds,
Below too, all calm, all vital and beautiful, and the farm prospers well.

Down in the fields all prospers well,
But now from the fields come father, come at the daughter's call,
And come to the entry mother, to the front door come right away.

Fast as she can she hurries, something ominous, her steps trembling,
She does not tarry to smooth her hair nor adjust her cap.

Open the envelope quickly,
O this is not our son's writing, yet his name is sign'd,
O a strange hand writes for our son, O stricken mother's soul!

All swims before her eyes, flashes with black, she catches the main words only,
Sentences broken, *gunshot wound in the breast, calvalry skirmish, taken to hospital,*
At present low, but will soon be better.

Ah now the single figure to me,
Amid all teeming and wealthy Ohio with all its cities and farms,
Sickly white in the face and dull in the head, very faint,
By the jamb of a door leans.

Grieve not so, dear mother, (the just-grown daughter speaks through her sobs,
The little sisters huddle around speechless and dismay'd,)
See, dearest mother, the letter says Pete will soon be better.

Alas poor boy, he will never be better, (nor may-be needs to be better, that brave and simple soul,)
While they stand at home at the door he is dead already,
The only son is dead.

But the mother needs to be better,
She with thin form presently drest in black,
By day her meals untouch'd, then by night fitfully sleeping, often waking,
In the midnight waking, weeping, longing with one deep longing,
O that she might withdraw unnoticed, silent from life escape and withdraw,
To follow, to seek, to be with her dear dead son.

Walt Whitman (1819–1892)

- The poem 'Come up from the Fields Father' tells a story. Write a summary of that story in five sentences.

- Both the poems 'A Wife in London' and 'Come up from the Fields Father' work by establishing a contrast between homelife and war. What effect does this contrast have on the reader?

- Re-write the ending of either 'Come up from the Fields Father' or 'A Wife in London' to make it positive. You will need to imitate the style of the poet, so look carefully at the poem you choose first.

- Compare and contrast the poems, 'A Wife in London' and 'Come up from the Fields Father'. What are the similarities and what are the differences? Think about the settings, the tone and the language the poets use.

Some of the war dead of the Battle of Antietam, American Civil War, 17 September 1862.

Gillian Clarke was born in Cardiff in 1937 and much of her poetry is about the Welsh countryside and rural life. 'The Field-Mouse' demonstrates how world events – in this case the Bosnian war – can impact on her life in Wales.

THE FIELD-MOUSE

Summer, and the long grass is a snare drum.
The air hums with jets.
Down at the end of the meadow,
far from the radio's terrible news,
we cut the hay. All afternoon
its wave breaks before the tractor blade.
Over the hedge our neighbour travels his field
in a cloud of lime, drifting our land
with a chance gift of sweetness.

The child comes running through the killed flowers,
his hands a nest of quivering mouse,
its black eyes two sparks burning.
We know it will die and ought to finish it off.
It curls in agony big as itself
and the star goes out in its eye.
Summer in Europe, the field's hurt,
and the children kneel in long grass,
staring at what we have crushed.

Before day's done the field lies bleeding,
the dusk garden inhabited by the saved, voles,
frogs, a nest of mice. The wrong that woke
from a rumour of pain won't heal,
and we can't face the newspapers.
All night I dream the children dance in grass
their bones brittle as mouse-ribs, the air
stammering with gunfire, my neighbour turned
stranger, wounding my land with stones.

Gillian Clarke (1937–   )

Children of Sarajevo ride on bicycles in a war-shattered suburb

- List all the references to
  - harvesting and Wales
  - Bosnia and war.

  How does Gillian Clarke connect these two, apparently different, things?

- Select two or three images for Wales and for Bosnia. Write an explanation of each, including details about how these relate to the wider issue of the poem.

- Write about this incident in the field as if you are one of the children. Imagine how a child would feel about the activity in general and the mouse in particular.

Do you believe that we are responsible for the world environment? Read the following poem. What do you think Gillian Clarke is saying about war and its impact on the environment and on ordinary people's lives?

LAMENT

For the green turtle with her pulsing burden,
in search of the breeding ground.
For her eggs laid in their nest of sickness.

For the cormorant in his funeral silk,
the veil of iridescence on the sand,
the shadow on the sea.

For the ocean's lap with its mortal stain.
For Ahmed at the closed border.
For the soldier in his uniform of fire.

For the gunsmith and the armourer,
the boy fusilier who joined for the company,
the farmer's sons, in it for the music.

For the hook-beaked turtles,
the dugong and the dolphin,
the whale struck dumb by the missile's thunder.

For the tern, the gull and the restless wader,
the long migrations and the slow dying,
the veiled sun and the stink of anger.

For the burnt earth and the sun put out,
the scalded ocean and the blazing well.
For vengeance, and the ashes of language.

Gillian Clarke (1937–)

Burning oil fields in Kuwait, Gulf War.

- Why is this poem called 'Lament'? What exactly is the poem lamenting?

- Select the images from this poem which are most striking for you. Design a poster to illustrate the message of this poem. You could include in your poster some of the important words and phrases which came to your attention when you were reading.

- Write a detailed analysis of the poem. Try to include comments on all the different aspects of poetry that you have covered in this book. Think about the structure, the tone and the imagery the poet uses.

COURSE WORK TITLES

The following tasks will give you opportunities to produce course work, or revise and develop what you have learned in this book.

- Many war poems consider the way war intrudes on peace and normal life-styles. Select two or three poems on this subject and explore the poets' thoughts and feelings.

  or

  How has the war interrupted the way of life of people in 'The Field-mouse' and 'As the Team's Head Brass'. Refer to the poems in detail.

- The landscape and nature are elements of life which are frequently present, even at moments of hardship and suffering. Discuss the presentation of nature in three of the following poems:

  'Sand' by John Jarmain

  'Returning, We Hear the Larks' by Isaac Rosenberg

  'The Hyaenas' by Rudyard Kipling

  'The Soldier' by Rupert Brooke

  'Fifty Faggots' by Edward Thomas

- Write about the way a sense of anger is conveyed in two or three poems on the subject of war. Explain fully what the poets' anger is directed at and how the poet conveys this anger.

  or

  Write about the feelings the poet has in two of the following poems:

  'The Hyaenas' by Rudyard Kipling

  'High Wood' by Philip Johnstone

  'Does it Matter?' by Siegfried Sassoon

  'Anthem for Doomed Youth' by Wilfred Owen

- Explore the imagery used in the poems 'Spring Offensive', 'Sand' and 'Returning, We Hear the Larks'. Refer specifically to the language the poets use.

  or

  Several of the poems you have studied tell a story. Select two or three poems and explain in detail the story that they tell and what the poem reveals about the nature of war.

- Many of the wars Great Britain has been involved in took place in other countries, but the effect they had was still profound. Discuss how 'life at home' and 'life at war' are presented in 'Route March Rest', 'Come up from the Fields Father' and 'Spring Offensive'.

  or

  How have the lives of the people been affected in the poems 'War Photographer', 'Drummer Hodge' and 'Disabled'?

- The voice of the poet is clearly heard in the poems 'Anthem for Doomed Youth', 'The Soldier' and 'Disabled'. What is it these poets are saying?

  or

  Select two or three poems which have made you react strongly. Explain how and why you have responded personally.

- Analyse the poetic style of either Thomas Hardy, Wilfred Owen, Gillian Clarke or Edward Thomas. (You may wish to use other poems not included in this book.)